MOO

A book of happiness for cow lovers

Compiled by Angus St John Galloway

EXISLE
PUBLISHING

Introduction

There are well over a billion cows in the world. Affectionate, playful, the cow is at the heart of many cultures. They have been with us through all our settled and 'civilized' years. So how we treat cattle is a full and fair measure of our values and our ability to live by them.

Cows represented one of the earliest forms of wealth, and in Greek, Egyptian and Hindu cultures they reached God-like status. For better or worse, we undoubtedly depend upon cows and today there is an increasing intolerance towards any ill treatment of these loving and inquisitive animals.

The growing popularity of the lifestyle block or hobby farm has put many of us in closer proximity to cows, while the increase in the number of rescue farms for ill-treated cattle and other farm animals has made more people aware that cows both matter and have feelings. As Alan Bennett said, 'Cows have far more awareness and know-how than they have ever been given credit for.'

There are hundreds of breeds of cattle; this book

features many of the more popular ones and a few other interesting ones besides. The quotes selected avoid bad-taste burger jokes and often reflect aspects of the human condition that also seem relevant to cows.

Cows make friends with other animals, including with humans and among themselves. They love their children, remember places, and are adaptable to changing situations. They are also determined, curious and know their own mind.

Cows are of course as diverse as humans. Some are tiny, but others from the hoof to the shoulder blades can reach nearly 2 metres (6½ feet), while some bulls can weigh well over a ton.

When we can see cows as distinct individuals — as all good famers of whatever scale do — we can enjoy their natures and appreciate that the animals we have been dependent upon for over 8000 years also have a lot of love, joy and companionship to share with us.

An idea that is not dangerous
is unworthy of being called
an idea at all.

OSCAR WILDE

A mother is always the beginning.
She is how things begin.

AMY TAN

All animals except man, know that the principal business of life is to enjoy it — and they do enjoy it as much as man and other circumstances will allow.

SAMUEL BUTLER

The seven good cows
are seven years,
and the seven good heads
of grain are seven years;
it is one and the same dream.

GENESIS 41:27

Moo may represent an idea,
but only the cow knows.

MASON COOLEY

A mother is a daughter's
best friend.

The cow is the purest
type of sub-human life.

MAHATMA GANDHI

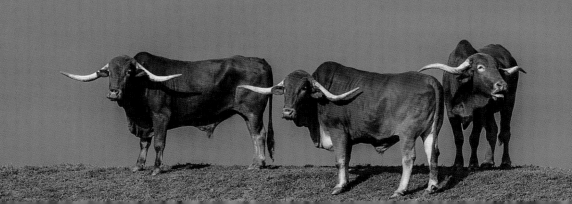

Somewhere in the depths of
my soul is the connection my
father had with his cattle.

CYRIL RAMAPHOSA

It was a silver cow. But when I say 'cow', don't go running away with the idea of some decent, self-respecting cudster such as you may observe loading grass into itself in the nearest meadow. This was a sinister, leering Underworld sort of animal, the kind that would spit out of the side of its mouth for twopence.

P.G. WODEHOUSE

Cows are as varied as people.
They can be highly intelligent
or slow to understand, vain
considerate and proud,
shy, or inventive.

ROSAMUND YOUNG

Milk contains growth hormones designed by Mother Nature to put a few hundred pounds on a baby calf within a few months.

MICHAEL GREGER

Cattle are noble animals,
and their keeping is a
noble endeavour.

PHILIP WALLING

Cows are gentle, interesting animals.

INGRID NEWKIRK

The horn is part of the
Longhorn's skull.

I paint from the top down.
From the sky, then the
mountains, then the hills, then
the houses, then the cattle and
then the people.

GRANDMA MOSES

Cows sometimes wear
an expression resembling
wonderment arrested on its way
to becoming a question.

FRIEDRICH NIETZSCHE

I've never run with the bulls.
I prefer to watch from the
safety of a balcony.

CESAR AZPILICUETA

I don't want to follow
the herd.

ALAIN ROBERT

Cows are the Devil's
handmaidens.

LINDA HOWARD

Trust but verify.

RONALD REAGAN

... This simple fact,
cows love each other.

ADAM NICOLSON
THE DAILY TELEGRAPH

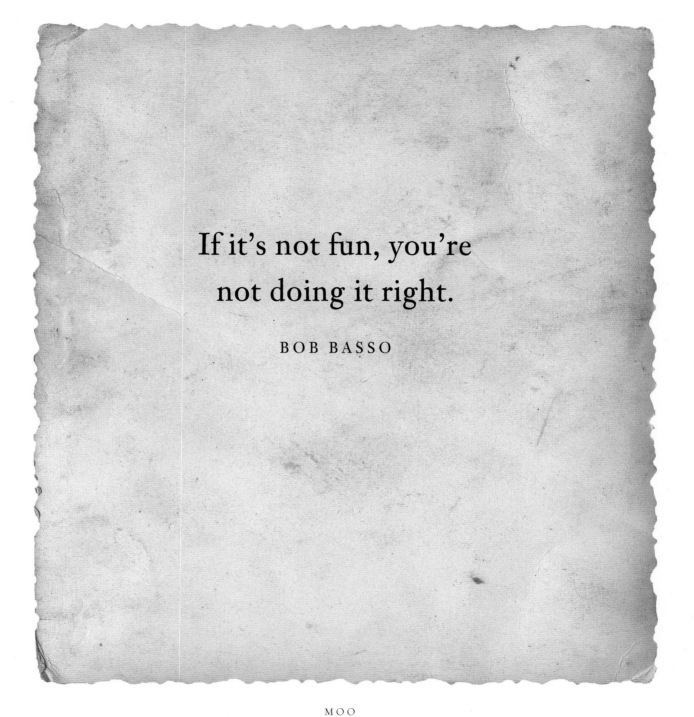

If it's not fun, you're
not doing it right.

BOB BASSO

A friend is someone who
knows all about you and
still loves you.

ELBERT HUBBARD

I was just sitting on the train,
just staring out of the window
at some cows. It was not
the most inspiring subject.
When all of a sudden,
the idea of Harry just
appeared in my mind's eye.

J.K. ROWLING

Studying cows, pigs and chickens can help an actor develop his character. There are a lot of things I learned from animals. One was that they couldn't hiss or boo me.

JAMES DEAN

He could tell by the way animals walked that they were keeping time to some kind of music. Maybe it was the song in their own hearts that they walked to.

LAURA ADAMS ARMER

Clearly, animals know more than
we think, and think a great deal
more than we know.

IRENE M. PEPPERBERG

I want you to see that I'm looking. Look at me look at you. I'm cool with that.

BUSTA RHYMES

Let everyone mind his own business and the cows will be well tended.

FRENCH PROVERB

I have no affinity for cows.
I mean, they're cool.

DOJA CAT

Every mind must make its choice between truth and repose. It cannot have both.

RALPH WALDO EMERSON

To every cow her calf,
to every book her copy.

ST COLUMBA

When hitting the horn of
a single cow, the horns of a
thousand cows hurt.

TYWA PROVERB

Let us remember that animals are not mere resources for human consumption. They are splendid beings in their own right, who have evolved alongside us as co-inheritors of all the beauty and abundance of life on this planet.

MARC BEKOFF

No historian or naturalist has ever so related an animal to the land, to men, and to history.

For each one of us stands alone
in the midst of a universe.

JOHN BUCHANAN ROBINSON

I like food. I like eating.
And I don't want to deprive
myself of good food.

SARAH MICHELLE GELLAR

Today we are searching for things in nature that are hidden behind the veil of appearance … We look for and paint this inner, spiritual side of nature.

FRANZ MARC

I've always thought the word cow was funny. And cows are sort of tragic figures. Cows blur the line between tragedy and humor.

GARY LARSON

The essence of cows is
their warmth, generosity,
stolidity, and sense of
peaceful contemplation.

VALERIE PORTER

When a Dalmatian sees a cow, he must be like 'What the hell happened to him?'... When the cow sees the Dalmatian, he must be like 'He looks amazing – I am so out of shape this is ridiculous.'

DEMETRI MARTIN

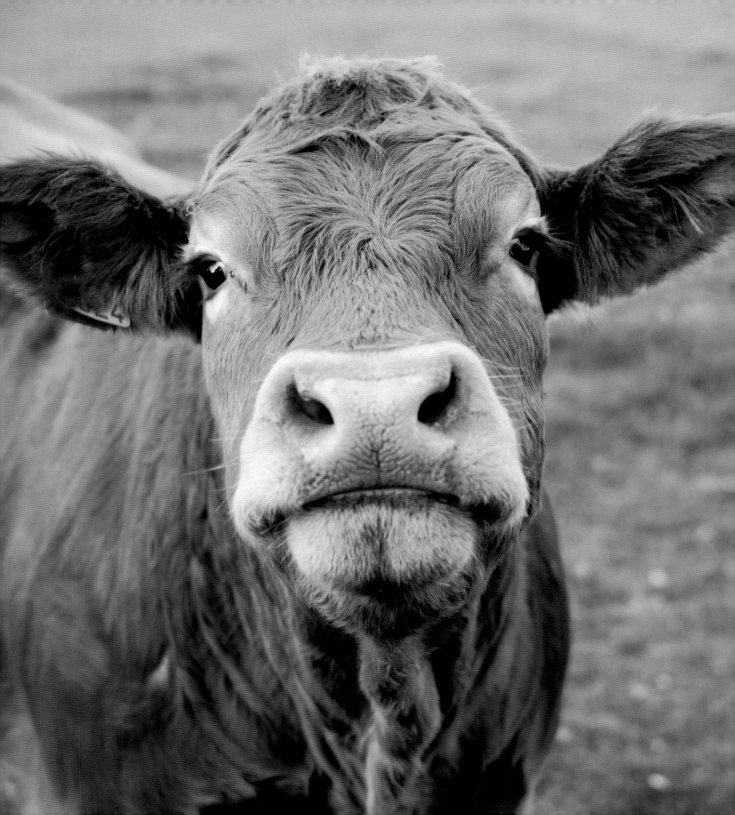

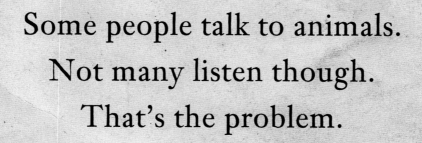

Some people talk to animals.
Not many listen though.
That's the problem.

A.A. MILNE

Gonna change my way
of thinking.

BOB DYLAN

My cow is not pretty but
it is pretty to me.

DAVID LYNCH

My mother is a walking miracle.

LEONARDO DICAPRIO

Animals are born who they
are, accept it, and that is that.
They live with greater peace
than people do.

GREGORY MAGUIRE

Do humans have a different moral
significance than cows in general?

RICHARD DAWKINS

A beach is not only a sweep of
sand, but shells of sea creatures,
the sea glass, the seaweed,
the incongruous objects washed
up by the ocean.

HENRY GRUNWALD

Cows are my passion. What
I have ever sighed for has been
to retreat to a Swiss farm and
live entirely surrounded by
cows — and china.

CHARLES DICKENS

A group of twelve or more cows
is called a flink.

Whenever I feel the need to exercise, I lie down until it goes away.

PAUL TERRY

I would not wish any companion
in the world but you.

SHAKESPEARE
THE TEMPEST

People who stare deserve
the looks they get.

MALCOLM FORBES

A question that sometimes
drives me hazy: am I or are the
others crazy?

ALBERT EINSTEIN

I love shifting between being
super cute and aggressive.
It's funny.

SIGRID

All that I am, or hope to be,
I owe to my angel mother.

ABRAHAM LINCOLN

Until one has loved an animal,
a part of one's soul remains
unawakened.

ANATOLE FRANCE

Things are never quite as scary
when you've got a best friend.

BILL WATTERSON

I am really rather like a beautiful jersey cow. I have the same pathetic droop to the corners of my eyes.

DEBORAH KERR

I go about looking at horses and cattle. They eat grass, make love, work when they have to, bear their young. I am sick with envy of them.

SHERWOOD ANDERSON

After climbing a great hill, one only finds that there are many more hills to climb.

NELSON MANDELA

Against the assault of
laughter, nothing can stand.

MARK TWAIN

Hope is a walk through a flowering meadow. One does not require that it lead anywhere.

ROBERT BREAULT

Cows are a lot smarter across
the board than bulls.

THOMAS HADEN CHURCH

Youth is beauty, even in cattle.

EGYPTIAN PROVERB

Cursed cows have
short horns.

CHINESE PROVERB

Total contentment is only for cows.

BETTE MIDLER

Hey, diddle, diddle,
the cat and the fiddle.
The cow jumped over the moon.

NURSERY RHYME

Life is an awful, ugly place to
not have a best friend.

SARAH DESSEN

Cows are our deities and
mountains and forests.

KRISHNA

Beware of him that is slow to anger;
for when it is long coming, it is the
stronger when it comes, and the longer
kept. Abused patience turns to fury.

FRANCIS QUARLES

Farmers should converse with a cow face-to-face if they want them to unwind, a new study suggests.

THE DAILY MAIL

Give every man thy ear,
but few thy voice.

SHAKESPEARE
HAMLET

There are few things better than falling asleep in a field and being woken up by an inquisitive cow.

MARY QUANT

Cows are amongst the gentlest
of breathing creatures:
none show more passionate
tenderness to their young …
I am not ashamed to profess a
deep love for these creatures.

THOMAS DE QUINCEY

The ancient Egyptians worshipped the life-giving, loving and often joyful Hathor — a Goddess of Life.

If having a soul means being able to feel love and loyalty and gratitude, then animals are better off than a lot of humans.

JAMES HERRIOT

Included Cow Breeds

Also in the Animal Happiness series

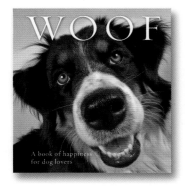

WOOF
A book of happiness for dog lovers

MEOW
A book of happiness for cat lovers

CLUCK
A book of happiness for chicken lovers

SPIRIT
A book of happiness for horse lovers

OINK
A book of fun for pig lovers

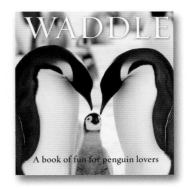

WADDLE
A book of fun for penguin lovers

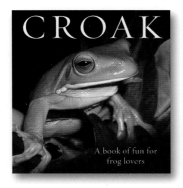

CROAK
A book of fun for frog lovers

BLEAT
A book of fun for goat lovers

BUZZ
A book of happiness for bee lovers

First published 2021
This edition published 2024

Exisle Publishing Pty Ltd
PO Box 864, Chatswood, NSW 2057, Australia
226 High Street, Dunedin, 9016, New Zealand
www.exislepublishing.com

A CiP record for this book is available from the
National Library of Australia.

ISBN 978 1 922539 82 3

Designed by Mark Thacker
Typeset in Archetype 24 on 36pt
Photographs courtesy of Shutterstock

Printed in China

This book uses paper sourced under ISO 14001 guidelines from
well-managed forests and other controlled sources.

2 4 6 8 10 9 7 5 3 1